LIVE UNTIL YOU DIE

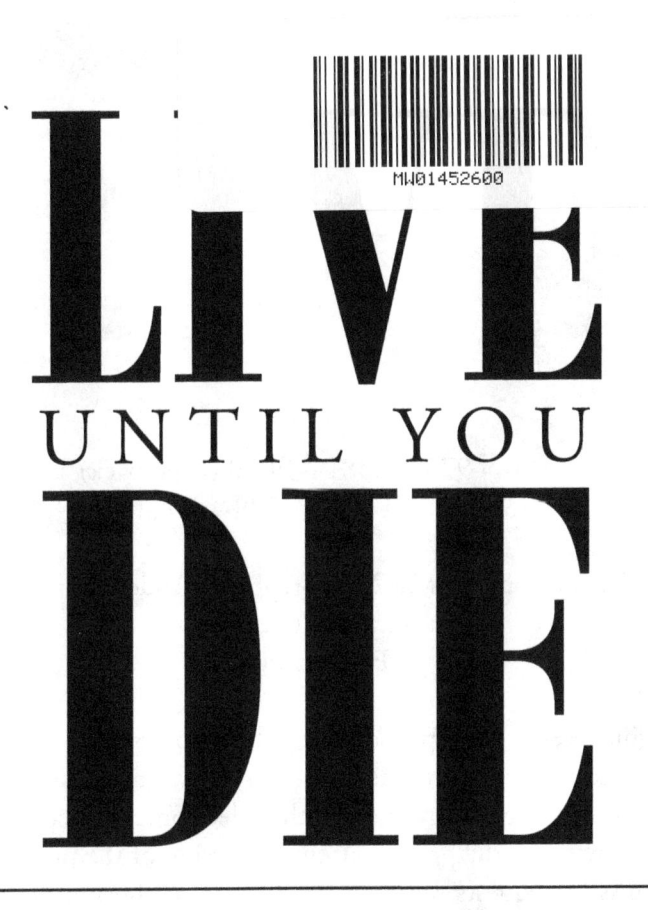

A Physician's Perspective on Fear and Uncertainty

Stephanie Anderson
MD, MBA

ISBN 978-1-63814-397-0 (Paperback)
ISBN 978-1-63814-399-4 (Digital)

Copyright © 2022 Stephanie Anderson
All rights reserved
First Edition

All rights reserved. No part of this publication may be reproduced, distributed, or transmitted in any form or by any means, including photocopying, recording, or other electronic or mechanical methods without the prior written permission of the publisher. For permission requests, solicit the publisher via the address below.

Covenant Books
11661 Hwy 707
Murrells Inlet, SC 29576
www.covenantbooks.com

FOREWORD

Dr. Stephanie Anderson offers the reader an opportunity to enter her world in a not so subtle or superficial manner in this wonderful piece, *Live Until You Die*. The title may cause one to infer that this is yet another self-help book. This would be a gross misinterpretation. In fact, I would describe the piece as a "self-less" book. Dr. Stephanie persistently challenges one to not think less of themselves but to think of themselves, and their desires less. This way of life and mode of thinking is contrary to contemporary culture, where a focus on self is paramount as social media often provides the vehicle for self-aggrandizement. While taking on an altruistic attitude, the reader is in the same breadth encouraged to embrace who they are unapologetically. Dr. Stephanie intentionally challenges the reader to view life through a different lens in the magnificent work, *Live Until You Die*.

The experience that one will feel while reading the book is a deeply personal one. We, the readers, are offered a look into what would normally be the most despondent point of a person's life, that being diagnosed with cancer. We are then allowed to experience her essentially direct encounter with God that is both startling and life-changing. In a way that only very few people that I have met can, Dr. Stephanie turns the table and uses such a low point in life to fuel a subsequent life of purpose and fulfillment. Her focus is shifted from the effect of such a diagnosis on her to how the diagnosis will affect her family and friends. Her focus shifts more to her perspective and less so on the circumstance while yet still maintaining self-care and self-love.

In a most captivating manner, Dr. Stephanie explains what victory really means in a time of uncertainty and inability to control the situation. The reader is challenged multiple times to go counterculture and accept that their life is not their own and that only when one accepts this premise will life be truly fulfilled. The reader is offered the clearest direction for the healing process and life change by simply succumbing to the process chosen not by us, but by the one who made us. Undoubtedly, many will feel uncomfortable with what is being proposed. But there is no growth without change and no change without pain or loss.

I owe a great deal of debt and gratitude to Dr. Stephanie, simply for being in my life. Her authenticity, tenacity, persistence, and willingness to always challenge me, continuously pushes me to be the best version of me I can. She often reminds me while referring to her own life situations that God's purpose for our life is not constant bliss and lack of trials. We are to embrace not only the mountaintop experiences but also the most difficult of challenges because they are all a part of HIS plan. As Dr. Stephanie explains to us in *Live Until You Die*, the serenity prayer should form our new perspective stating, "God, grant me the serenity to accept the things I cannot change, courage to change the things I can, and wisdom to know the difference."

An excerpt from chapter four embodies my life to this very day, "I am who I am today because of the advantages and challenges of living life, I am where I am today because of them, I love the way I love today because of them, and I give the way I give today because of them." I challenge each of you to make your life about something bigger than yourself. Give more of your time, energy, effort, riches, and grace in order to live the fulfilled life you are meant to have. Remember, life in some respects is similar to a savings and loan bank. Life will give you what you request or desire, but there will come a time when you will be asked to repay it and often with interest. It is no mistake if one gives more than they receive. That is the definition of a fulfilled life.

Frederick D. Johnson, Jr., MD
Thomasville, Georgia

INTRODUCTION

Life has a funny way of showing us what we need to know, as well as what we should try to avoid. It happens without our permission, and sometimes is a consequence of our decisions and choices. The cycle of life can repeat itself from one generation to the next, but we possess the power and capability to break generational disadvantages and fortify generational advantages. We are in a constant battle of making ourselves into what has been defined as a picture of success but the question remains, "Who's the author of the picture?"

We share ideas and thoughts on a daily basis, curating our images into what is an expected norm while dismissing the inner voice of our distinctiveness, individuality, and identity. What if you were not designed to be just like your mother, father, brother, sister, neighbor, friend, boss, athlete, actor, musician, politician, or anyone else that you may idealize? What if you were only created to be you, indescribable, unapologetic, exuberant, and expressively sound with a special landing place?

Your past and present are preparing you for your destiny. Passion produces a burden for what we were created to accomplish while living here on earth. If we were able to know what our futures hold, then our choices would be guided by lots of care and concern. When we stop asking the question of ourselves to be just like everyone else and embrace who we are while respecting differences, we give others permission to take off their mask and be themselves as well. Living past fear is the greatest gift you will ever give to yourself, your family, your friends, and the world.

CHAPTER 1

Understanding the Fear Factor

Fear is defined as an unpleasant emotion caused by the belief that someone or something is dangerous, likely to cause pain or a threat. We are often fearful of what we have never experienced, cannot control, or do not understand. As children, we are equipped to be fearless, learning new things daily, and experimenting with endless opportunities without doubt or constraint. Research has shown the first five years are especially crucial for physical, intellectual, and social-emotional development as children. Fear does not inhibit their potential progression for awfully long, they learn to roll, crawl, cruise, walk, and then run while making painful mistakes along the way. Children may cry some tears and receive bumps and bruises, but the anticipation of the discomfort does not prevent them from trying again.

If we were to grasp situations and circumstances through a child's perspective, I believe the actual unpleasant emotion caused by our belief would be short-lived, just like the effect of a parental threat of discipline for misbehavior. If we grab hold of our beliefs and position them towards a positive expectation; we have won half the battle. Our emotions and reactions usually follow our assumptions and expectations. Have you ever experienced your heart and mouth echoing two different expressions? Positioning our beliefs towards a positive projection is what I would call paying it forward, meaning your faith springing your emotions into an undeniable mode of accepting. It does not matter if an outcome is favorable or not, it will still all work out for my good.

Acceptance does not mean negating hurt, anger, frustration, disappointment, or sadness; it simply promotes an attitude of something that is happening which is beyond my control. Experiencing feelings about situations and people does not change our propensity to become an overcomer; we all share moments of not being accepting of what is happening to or around us, but the facts still remain the same. We often find ourselves in positions of discomfort, challenge, or counterproductivity;

these have sometimes proven to be life-enhancing moments, which refine our character by stretching our motivation, intentions, understanding, and abilities to new heights and depths that we didn't even think were possible.

The facts may be dreadful but the truth can remain the same, I am more than this situation, circumstance, person, or challenge that is causing a disruption in my everyday life, although it may cause some pain and discomfort, I will be a better person who is passionate about my life and influencing my environment. Once we understand the motivation of our fear, we can make an intelligent decision to regress, become stagnate, or move forward.

When we are faced with the possibility of something being wrong or is wrong, our mind and body naturally begin to react. I recall the initial concern of feeling something abnormal in my right breast, it was not until two months later, after receiving a confirmed diagnosis of breast cancer that my body and mind began to react. The nurse practitioner called to ask me to come into the office, I politely told her I'm a physician, and I have to be at work in two hours, so I know that means something is abnormal, please go ahead and tell me. She said,

"Your biopsy showed DCIS (Ductal Carcinoma in Situ)."

I said, "Okay, I am going to military training for two weeks and I will see you guys upon completion for an appointment." The news was both a relief and a game changer, I was happy that I was not crazy, and identified something that was legitimately wrong but understood that my life would never be the same. Needless to say, my shift in the ED that night was long, and I did a lot of research. In my quiet time, I begin to ponder the effect of this information on my family and not necessarily myself.

My cousin who was forty-eight years old had been diagnosed with cholangiocarcinoma seven months before I received my diagnosis, after a courageous battle and aggressive chemotherapy, she went home to be with the Lord the day after I received my diagnosis. After watching her journey of being laid off from a company she had worked for over twenty years, then having a year off where she enjoyed extensive travel and spending time with family and friends before starting a new job; somehow, I find comfort in what God allowed her to do with her time on earth. She touched and encouraged so many lives and her legacy continues today with a scholarship fund, blog, and auto dealership.

In retrospect, she prepared me for my experience by her bravery and fortitude. It is not easy to focus on your own challenge when a death has occurred and you are grieving with your family. Strength comes when we least expect it and kicks fear in the butt. Sometimes, the very challenge that prompts a flight or fight response in us saves us from ourselves, every day above ground is another day to make a difference. Fear can only become what we allow it to become, it can only stay where we encourage it to dwell, and it can only be productive if we do not replace it with faith.

Reflection Questions:

1. What challenges or situations have you faced that cause you to become fearful?

   _____

2. How did you respond to that feeling of being afraid, was it positive or negative?

   _____

3. What motivates you during tough situations and how do you process what is happening to you?

   _____

4. How can you create a meaningful way to express yourself to others during your times of uncertainty?

   _____

5. Do you have someone you can trust to listen without judgment and advise when necessary in order to gain an alternative perspective?

   _____

CHAPTER 2

Understanding the New Reality

As young minds, we have dreams about how our lives should be, our job, our spouse, our children, our daily routine, our home, our friends, and our measure of success. As we grow older, life experiences and school have the tendency to teach us the difference between fantasy and reality. We go through life, learning while adding bits and pieces to our vision for life from experiences and observations. We watch television shows and movies, follow friends and family on social media, depicting the script of life from the mind of a novelist creator.

Somehow, thinking this is how life is supposed to be, enchanting and thrilling with plot twisters and happy ever after endings all the time. We adopt expectations and revelations concerning our being and doing while creating a mental vision board for the future. We take suggestions and advice from others as authoritative subject matter experts without considering the obvious realism; their journey may be different and unique, requiring different choices, assumptions, anticipations, and ultimately outcomes.

Similarly, we have an expectation that we will always be in good health with great mobility; diseases, trauma, and accidents may happen to others but definitely not to me. Then one day, you hear some unexpected news which changes your thoughts, dreams, family, and way of life immediately. You have cancer, heart disease, diabetes, kidney failure, any other medical/mental process, or you are pregnant; a family member, child, or friend has an untimely death or a life-altering experience; there has been a natural disaster such as a tornado, hurricane, earthquake, fire, etc., or worse there has been a terrorist attack or bombing affecting the way we perform daily routines and liberties. Perhaps a trivial incident caused demise or missing persons due to a mechanical or operational failure during a routine activity. All these things can affect our lives in a momentous manner with little to no time to respond.

I believe we start with the denial process, whatever was heard or said can't be true, the medical center must have mixed up my results with someone else, my family or friend was just here this morning, children are not supposed to die before their parents, my job should be loyal to me and have not let me go; I thought I was in control of my life! I cannot have whatever that person with a medical degree told me, the x-rays, CT scan, and lab work are wrong. It is hard to grasp something extra or unexpected is happening in the one body you get to occupy on earth.

If you are familiar with the diagnosis, a spirit of catastrophizing may overwhelm your thoughts. If you know very little or nothing at all, so many personal questions invade your mind and you may feel inadequate because you do not really know what you want to ask for clarity. These are hard places to maneuver, life as you know it begins to flash before your eyes. So many questions: Will I be okay? Will I see my children/grandchildren celebrate life milestones? Who will take care of my babies? I cannot afford to be sick; I do not have health insurance. Will someone have to take care of me? Will I be able to continue working? Who will be my support channel? Did I make this happen by neglecting my health or making poor choices?

There are some challenges in life, which we have no control over, while there are others, which are the results of our choices. Hearing the words, you have cancer, instantly changed my world. I first needed to understand the type and options for treatment, then I was better equipped to make some informed decisions. For me being a child of God, my faith immediately reminded me of all the things God has brought me through and this too shall pass, and my victory is not determined by being healed or not, but by God's supreme will for my life. If He heals me and I don't ever have to worry about this again, great, but if he allows me to go on this journey and the end result is me leaving this world to spend eternal life with Him, it's still a win.

I firmly believe God has my best interest at heart. Trust me when I say, I did not develop this peace or faith in God overnight, I have been through many trials and tribulations where my response was not so calm. Life's hopefulness has taught me as long as there is still breath in my body, I have another chance to get it right or continue in the same direction. All challenges are not designed to cause destruction, sometimes pressure brings out our best character, motivation, and tenacity.

My new reality began the day of surgery, I chose a bilateral mastectomy with reconstruction because mentally, I did not want to have to question, what if it comes back or happens on the other side? I chose reconstruction because I still want to be cute and besides, my husband has not found me yet. I am so serious but yet joking; humor keeps me grounded and happy.

Let me be clear, I do believe that the man God has for me will love me with or without breasts because who we are consists of so much more than our appearance. We all have some vain thoughts about ourselves at one time or another, the key is to love yourself just the way you are, and give others permission to love you as well. The resolution to making the most out of a situation, good, bad, or indifferent is to dissect the possibilities, be honest with yourself, and consider what will give you the most peace. Our choices for treatment or lack thereof will not be the same, because everyone has a different set of circumstances. It is okay to choose what is best for you despite the wishes of your healthcare provider, family, and friends.

How do we dissect the possibilities? First, we must consider what is the problem, event, or process that we were not given a choice to deal with and how does this affects us and our livelihood. We must understand the realm of challenges with the change that must take place while realizing that we can only dictate so much if anything at all. If we are not familiar with the problem, process, or potential outcomes; we must gain the right knowledge, and not be afraid to ask questions and for time to ponder thoughts, feelings, anxieties, and concerns. Being honest with ourselves is usually easier said than done, we are sometimes our worst critics. This can prevent us from processing feelings, expectations, and options properly.

We all want to be strong and independent to a certain extent, being vulnerable is not a weakness, it is human and necessary for connecting with others. You don't have to share all your business with everyone, but please have an inner circle of family and/or friends that you can discuss your fears, doubts, grievances, incomprehension, denial, and whatever else you may want to get off your chest. These feelings can be totally normal, it would be a mistake to keep them in a bottle. After sharing with yourself and giving yourself permission to feel, then you can make the best choice for your situation. This may take a few conversations with some loved ones and professionals, but ultimately you have to be the one who understands the effect, consequences, and outcomes of your decision.

I went from working, mowing the lawn, house chores, vehicle maintenance, working out, and going out to breakfast to lying in bed with no breasts and two drains sticking out, one on each side. I became totally dependent on my family and friends to care for me. I do not think anything or anyone could have prepared me for this new reality. Knowing what to expect was one thing, but actually experiencing these changes is where the rubber met the road. So many thoughts raced through my mind because all I had time to do was think and appreciate my wonderful caretakers. I was trying to be a good patient, but also doing as much as possible to limit the burden on my caretakers. It was hard to switch from the physician role to the dependent patient who could not raise her arms above ninety degrees or lift anything.

Accepting my new way of being and doing was helpful to keep me sane. I actually began to appreciate slowing down and having time to spend with family and friends. If we spend our mental, emotional, and physical energy, and efforts appreciating what we do have and are capable of doing, then what we may not be able to do seems incomparable. One young lady explained it best after becoming wheelchair-bound at twenty-six years old, secondary to a stroke. She said the wheelchair does not limit her: it actually gives her the freedom to go anywhere she desires. You see, it is all about our perspective, not necessarily our circumstances.

Reflection Questions:

1. What dreams do you have for your life that have been put on hold by circumstances beyond your control?

   _____

2. Think of a challenge or circumstance that presented itself in your life, in retrospect, how could you improve handling the situation?

   _____

3. List your inner circle and connect with them by written form or verbally to show your appreciation.

   _____

4. What resources, methods, or habits do you use to keep yourself at a place of serenity?

   _____

5. Are you a person, you would want to come to for support and comfort during difficult times?

   _____

Chapter 3

Accepting the New Reality and It Changes

God, grant me the Serenity
To accept the things I cannot change…
Courage to change the things I can,
And Wisdom to know the difference.
Living one day at a time,
Enjoying one moment at a time,
Accepting hardship as the pathway to peace.
Taking, as He did, this sinful world as it is,
Not as I would have it.
Trusting that He will make all things right
if I surrender to His will.
That I may be reasonably happy in this life,
And supremely happy with Him forever in the next.
Amen

—*Reinhold Niebuhr*

The serenity prayer is in our hearts, in our minds, on our walls, and recited many times when we find ourselves in disturbing times or situations. Most of us are remarkably familiar with the first stanza and have used those words for comfort through some tough life experiences. Living everyday life and working countless hours in emergency rooms, clinics, and volunteering with local organizations has taught me that acceptance is a choice, not necessarily a feeling. There is usually a constant battle between our mind, heart, and soul, which may prevent us from desiring to give full attention to a necessary matter.

The Bible says, "A good man out of the good treasure of his heart bringeth forth that which is good; and an evil man out of the evil treasure of his heart bringeth forth that which is evil: for of the abundance of the heart his mouth speaketh" (Luke 6:45 KJV). What resonates in our hearts will proceed from our lips, we must become mindful, and slow down in some situations. The ability to constructively process what has happened, is happening, or may happen can help us with acceptance. There are so many things we cannot change; however, we have endless opportunities to create an alternate and fulfilling perspective.

One of my neighbors spoke a profound truth as she was sharing the story of her childhood and her mother committing suicide when she was fifteen years old; she expressed how too often people use their given circumstances as excuses to not be or do any better as a person or in life. We sometimes find ourselves clinging to an experience, which encourages hopelessness while denying the power to move forward.

Just as I settled into the fact of not having my own breasts and accepted that my life should return to some sense of normalcy in about six months, I had a follow-up appointment and my pathology report had positive margins with 2 foci of invasive ductal carcinoma, HER 2 positivity, and ER positivity. What did this mean? My oncologist was unsure, so I had the opportunity to visit two radiation oncologists, consult with one of the two breast specialists in the area, and visit another hematology oncologist. Not what I planned or expected, my simple plan of surgery and recovery had now turned into recommendations for chemotherapy, radiation, and immunotherapy. What was thought to be a simple case of DCIS had now become complicated without a proven management plan.

Every specialist I spoke to shared a different opinion about what was best for me. I thought to myself if you cannot agree with each other, why should I agree with you? Let me be clear, I am so grateful and appreciative of all my healthcare providers and staff. As I am fully aware, the art of medicine is not a one size fits all, it takes time, research, and careful consideration for each individual's state of affairs. Although I became frustrated with the never-ending visits and countless recommendations, I am confident that each person devised a management plan that was believed to be in my best interest.

Now, my six-month return to normal plan had increased to potentially being off for over a year. But wait, in the midst of preparing for reconstruction after radiation therapy, the coronavirus pandemic has come upon us. This unexpected turn of events helped me decide not to return to the emergency department until the completion of immunotherapy, which will be a total of sixteen months after surgery.

I quickly learned with the diagnosis of breast cancer and the pandemic of coronavirus, some things are beyond our control and we must trust God and go with the flow from one day to the next. The interesting thing is seeing it happen to everyone at once with the coronavirus pandemic, nothing is as it was and the future has become unknown. We are constantly on a roller coaster of change, which is determined by infected people and their deaths. Families are forced to spend uninterrupted quality time together, schools have been closed for the year, financial struggles are ensuing due to lack of work, churches have been closed, and we have been ordered to stay in our houses.

When did we ever expect this to be our lives today? Never would probably be the right answer, but the question remains, "Will things become different as this crisis dissipates?" Will family bonds become stronger or be torn apart? Will our priorities and values change or remain the same? Will we financially prepare ourselves from the unexpected? Will we begin to trust God in every aspect of our lives? What will we think is important? Will politics, social economics, or brand matter? There are so many unanswered questions, but our new reality will hopefully revolutionize our world and lives as we know it.

Standing on the promises of hope, love, faith, and trust gives us more excitement than concern about what is currently happening. The facts do not always represent the truth of the matter, we must embrace what is happening behind the scenes. Change happens for multiple reasons, to give us something, to take something, or to help us reevaluate who and where we are; understanding the reasoning for the change is key to accepting the lesson to be learned from the change. Our feelings about change are not always favorable, we constantly want to feel as if we are in control. The truth is we are not, I have come to understand that my life is not my own and have peace with God's will for me.

Did I always feel this way? Of course not, we all have plans for our lives from the time we can think to have plans for our dream spouse, house, job, children, hobbies, vacation, etc. I never planned to have breast cancer; however, I am so thankful for this journey, I have been blessed to embrace it to the fullest possible extent. I have had so much more time to do things with family and friends, take a pause and breath, learn God's love on a whole new level, and remain open to his plans for my life. I do not feel as if I have failed my successful plan, but I understand that there has been a detour from my expected plan and I have become welcoming of whatever is next. Acceptance does not necessarily take away frustration, hurt, anger, disappointment, or fear but it does allow us to become open to healing and wholeness, which may pave the way for our next successful chapter in life.

Reflection Questions:

1. How do you handle situations which are beyond your control?

   _____

2. Do you encounter judgmental or fear-based reactions from people when you share your struggles and challenges? If so, how does that feel?

   _____

3. We often struggle with the concept of being in control. We think we should be better at making things and people respond the way we expect. But is trying to control circumstances or people really accepting them for their authentic self?

   _____

4. What is one thing that you wish you could do differently when you find yourself in unforeseen circumstances?

   _____

5. After reading this chapter, what patterns or stigmas in your mindset are you questioning?

   _____

CHAPTER 4

The Impact of a New Reality

In our world today, there have been so many events, from the Apollo 11 moon landing to Coronavirus and everything before and in between, which constantly impact our reality and are integral parts in shaping our lives and history. Despite our differences in generational gaps, ethnic background, nationality, genders, political affiliations, socioeconomic status, etc.; there have been life-altering experiences whether directly or indirectly influencing our everyday life.

One that comes to mind easily is the terrorist attacks on September 11, 2001. Everyone usually remembers what they were doing that day; we had approximately three thousand people who lost their lives, comprised of citizens from seventy-eight countries and over two-thousand six hundred who sustained injuries. 9/11 alone changed the way we protect our country, the Department of Homeland

Security was designed, it also contributes to the longest war in American history in Afghanistan. It significantly impacted our economy with job loss, massive repair and recovery costs, and victim compensation funds due to health-related issues surrounding 9/11. There are so many heroes, front line workers, survivors, and families that live daily with the impact of those tragic events mentally, physically, emotionally, and financially. I am grateful and appreciative for those who sacrificed so much for us to live a life of freedom today.

Lives are changed when we become selfless and yield to the process chosen for us without bitterness and anger. It is hard to grasp the concept of reaping and sowing in the wake of challenges, disappointments, and anguish. Sometimes, the healing process is accelerated by shifting our focus on someone else's challenges and being in a position to provide encouragement and support. It is amazing how small issues and circumstances become when you listen and empathize with someone else's story or struggle. I have learned that my perspective determines my outlook and response to whatever is happening in life. I refuse to allow any challenge, situation, or person to hold me hostage when there are so many more meaningful things to do.

During my treatment appointments, I have had the opportunity to meet wonderful people every time I visited an office, hospital, or treatment center. Many of their stories have impacted my life and career. I have developed a new respect for patients and their considerations for a management plan. You see, as a physician in practice, I did not have time to hear the patients and all their concerns. As a fellow patient, I get to hear other's experiences, concerns, and fears with precision and resolve. Unfortunately, we as physicians are not always given a fair amount of time to accomplish all our assigned tasks in a day, this can ultimately lead to ineffective communication and patient dissatisfaction. Many of us do the best we can and hope to serve our patients to the best of our ability, which hopefully accomplishes the best healthcare choices and healthy opportunities to promote a long and fulfilling life.

As we are still facing challenges from the effects of COVID-19, many people are becoming frantic while making demands, which may not be in their best interest and could potentially lead to a fatal outcome. Many are acting out in frustration and outrage, requesting actions from the government for freedom despite the risk of contracting a fatal virus. The reality is we have no control over the next day or moment, we are not able to make plans for trips, shopping, sports, dancing, vacations, or even church activities; we are confined to a new normal.

We are now entering the time for children to return to school. Parents are having to make tough choices, whether their children should go to school or attend virtually. Some parents are struggling to make ends meet due to lost wages, family ties are being strained with the additional stress of social limitations. We are enduring a time in life when there is not a one size fits all approach, our routine system and processes have been thrown into a state of disarray. We develop mental images of how things should go in our lives, however, we never consider a contingency plan for the interruptions along the way while enjoying the journey of life.

If we consider everything we have dealt with and situations that have presented themselves along the way, I do not know about you, but I am thankful for some of those interruptions. Despite the devastation of 9/11, there were also some positive effects, heightened security measures especially with air travel, military support and opportunities, a greater focus on family life, higher church attendance, and increased expressions of patriotism. I am who I am today because of the advantages and challenges of living life, I am where I am today because of them, I love the way I love today because of them, and I give the way I give today because of them. No one ever promised me an easy life, but I have learned some important lessons from my parents, family, and friends; go with the flow when it is beyond your control.

We cannot change what is happening to us, but we can determine the effect it will have on our lives. We are not lone rangers living in a world of isolation, we always have a Father who cares for us even when we choose the wrong path or encounter obstacles. Our reality changes from day to day by one simple action, behavior, or thought, sometimes, it changes without our permission or intention; however, we still have a choice to make our circumstances the best or worst thing that has ever happened to us.

Reflection Questions:

1. Think of a historical event that has had a lasting impact on your life, recall how you felt about it initially. Do you still feel the same way or has your perspective blossomed from the lessons of the event?

_____

2. What challenges have you endured in life? Who are you today because of those challenges?

   _____

3. What advantages have you received in life? Who are you today because of the advantages?

   _____

4. Are there any potential obstacles or situations that could cause a drastic change in your daily life? If so, is there anything you can change today to decrease the chance of that incident from happening?

   _____

5. Who have you been able to influence because of your challenges or advantages?

   _____

5
CHAPTER

Embracing a New Reality

We have so many aspects of life to consider when things are changing around us, do we continue the same job, live in the same place, go to the same school, keep the same relationships, continue the same budget, or continue the same work-life balance? Ultimately, the question is, do we remain the same in our thoughts, speech, efforts, dreams, and daily activities. I am constantly reminded of the serenity prayer: *God, grant me the serenity to accept the things I cannot change, courage to change the things I can, and wisdom to know the difference.* These words have changed my perspective as well as others during many moments of uncertainty.

Our words determine our motivation to continue or change. Sometimes, we are thrown off by so many external factors, challenges, and circumstances that we forget to remember what we have spoken to ourselves according to the promises that we have been given through our heavenly father. To a certain extent, we shall have what we say and will become what we speak. If we are constantly speaking doubt and defeat, eventually, it may begin to manifest in our lives. Likewise, if we speak victory and overcoming, it may begin to manifest in our behaviors and actions.

No one knows you better than you, so learn how to motivate and encourage yourself. Too often, we walk around with insecurities which lead us to value others' opinion more than God's, or our own. We create opportunities to be less authentic and influential than we were created to be. Who is looking back at you in the mirror? We are all wonderfully and marvelously made to be unique, special, and one of a kind, our ability to embrace any obstacle that life throws our way is based upon our foundation, truths, and values.

A wonderful lady I met during radiation, who has been married for over thirty years received the life-changing diagnosis of having lung cancer with metastasis to her brain only three months before I met her, and was told her prognosis is poor and she has a maximum of approximately three years left to live. She was so excited about life and all that she wanted to accomplish before she leaves this world. She shared her bucket list with me, their plans to consolidate living expenses with her daughter, and cashing in life insurance policies to pay their house off. She is quilting a blanket with pictures for her grandchild since she may not make her wedding day. She also told her husband how she wants to celebrate their thirty-year anniversary just in case she is no longer with us.

She expressed that initially, she was saddened by her diagnosis and prognosis, but then she realized it was not going to limit the life she has left, so she has decided to live every day to the fullest. She also shared that her family did not appreciate her candid conversations about what may happen concerning her health and eventually death; but she stated, "I want them to be prepared and know my wishes."

I am amazed at this lady's courage, strength, and optimistic attitude, so I probed a little further about her faith and what led her to this transforming conclusion. She responded by saying they had not found a church they like in the city, but she does her own devotionals at home and loves the Lord. She moved to our city to receive treatment and spend quality time with her family. Clearly, this amazing woman had accepted a new reality with a positive attitude while choosing to make the most out of her remaining moments on earth.

Love and acceptance do not take on any certain form, it is unpredictable and can lead us on an emotional roller coaster. We sometimes place stock and value in so many things, money, jobs, houses, status, vehicles, travel, investment, etc.; but sometimes we miss the moments that really count. During my time working with hospice and palliative care and also in emergency medicine, no one has ever expressed wishing they had more time to make money, work, or travel; usually, they are desiring to have spent more time with their family and friends, listened more intently, loved more deeply, cared differently for close ones who have already passed, shared more moments making memories, and shared all their heart feels about the people in their life.

Life is precious and unforeseeable, it is so important to live each day as if it is your last. Please do not have regrets, animosity, or unaccomplished aspirations because you are thinking there will always be tomorrow. We are experiencing some unprecedented times, so many have had their tomorrows taken away by coronavirus, natural disasters, health issues, and unfortunate acts of violence. Yes, life is happening and we have responsibilities, however, we also have an obligation to love without restraint.

Sometimes, we need a little time and a lot of patience to help our perspective blossom into a peace that surpasses all understanding, giving us a little glimpse of joy, concerning a heartbreaking situation. My aunt and cousin have both expressed gratitude and peace, knowing that my cousin who died did not have to be alone during hospitalizations or chemotherapy treatments. If she was still physically here with us today, times would be hard for her and the family, no one wants to suffer alone and no family members want to hear you cannot see your daughter, sister, niece, or aunt because we are trying to prevent exposure to coronavirus.

Love transcends death, but our minds have a hard time grasping the inability to show affection, care, and concern for a beloved family member. There are so many people who have had to suffer and die alone, my hope is they felt the love, care, concern, and warmth of their family and friends' embrace, although they may have been miles away. Wouldn't it be amazing, if we are able to adjust our everyday normal to make others feel like they are special, appreciated, and loved?

Reflection Questions:

1. Considering all your life lessons, blessing, and challenges, knowing what you know now, is there anything you would have advised your younger self to do differently?

   _____

2. Make a list of people who can benefit from your lessons learned during this journey of life and connect with them. How can you make your relationship flourish?

   _____

3. What methods, strategies, or processes do you use to help you embrace the unknown and unforeseeable challenges?

   _____

4. How do you identify when you have peace concerning a situation?

   _____

5. If you only had six months left on earth, what would you do the same and what would you do differently?

_____

CONCLUSION

Finishing Your Course

We have all been given a timeline to live life on earth for some it is short and sweet, while others have a longer length of time. Quantity of time does not seem to matter as much as the quality of time; so many people have missed opportunities to be great for themselves and their families. We see life as something we should accomplish rather than a state of being and enjoying each and every precious moment. I had a dream or vision many years ago. I was walking into a building where there was a casket upfront, so I assumed it was a funeral, there were so many people, flowers, and tears. As I walked up to pay my respects to the deceased and view the body, I realized the person lying in the casket was me. I began to shake and cry uncontrollably because I did not understand why I was seeing my own funeral.

God begins to speak to me and ask, "Did you accomplish all that you should have while you were alive, did you impact the lives that you were destined too, did you use your time wisely or did you act selfishly and become all that you thought you should be rather than what I destined you to be?" I was humbled instantly with tears and sobbing; my life was submitted to God, but somehow, I had gotten off course. I needed a reminder, it is so easy to play the victim when life challenges you to your very core, but God is faithful and a rewarder of those who diligently seek him. The tribulations of life may not be fair, but all things work together for the good of those who love the Lord and are called according to his purpose.

We were never promised a comfortable life, a loving family, respectable kids, the perfect job, or no health challenges, but we are given hope in the midst of each and every crisis. If we could really grasp and understand as James proclaimed, counting it all as joy, this means standing in the pain, hurt, trial, disappointment, or challenge with an attitude of expectation. The purpose of the process will be worthwhile, although the process of pruning is uncomfortable, the end result will be God being glorified and my life and circumstances in a much better realm of the living. It is easy to discount a process while it is ongoing, we continue to see change day after day; if we exercise our faith and stand on the truth of God, we accept his outcomes and his timing.

It is my sincere desire and prayer that you are embracing your journey with a sensational attitude of hope and joy! Our lives will continue to change daily with and without our permission, it becomes a choice to make the most out of each and every situation. You are more than your past, environment, and circumstances; live each day with an expectation of gratitude and show this world exactly who you are!

ABOUT THE AUTHOR

Stephanie Anderson, MD, MBA is a board-certified family and emergency medicine physician. She is a servant at heart, philanthropist, speaker, writer, consultant, resilience trainer, soldier, actor, athlete, and advocate for underserved populations, children, and the elderly. She is the founder of https://purposefortoday.com where she connects, inspires, and learns from others while sharing a blogger's platform. She is passionate about showing God's love to others through personal and professional mentoring and coaching, ministry, medicine, and living everyday life. She currently resides in Tennessee, where she practices as an independent contractor. *To find out more about Stephanie, or book her for a project or event, connect on Facebook @purposefortoday8, or LinkedIn*, or contact her by email at stephanie.andersonmd@gmail.com

CPSIA information can be obtained
at www.ICGtesting.com
Printed in the USA
JSHW041201200522
26053JS00002B/101

9 781638 143970